PRESENTED TO

_____

FROM

_____

DATE

_____

SINGLE

INSPIRATIONAL
MEDITATIONS

AGAIN

AND

SECURE

IN

GOD'S
LOVE

JIM SMOKE

J. COUNTRYMAN
NASHVILLE, TENNESSEE

Published by J. Countryman ®, a division of Thomas Nelson, Inc.,
Nashville, Tennessee 37214

Published in association with the literary agency of
Alive Communications, 1465 Kelly Johnson Blvd., Suite 320,
Colorado Springs, Colorado 80920

J. Countryman ® is a trademark of Thomas Nelson Inc.

Project editor: Jenny Baumgartner

Designed by Identity Design, Dallas, Texas
Illustrations © by Larry Moore

ISBN 0-8499-5704-4

Printed and bound in U.S.A.

EVERY
MORNING is
A FRESh
beginning.

DAN CUSTER

CONTENTS

SHOCKED! ANGRY! DAZED! BITTER! EMPTY! HURT! CHEATED! REJECTED!

*T*hese, along with an assortment of other feelings, probably describe how you are feeling if you have separated from a marriage that began with optimism, happiness, and hope. A terrible thing that somehow always happened to "other people" is happening to you. There is little if any preparation for the chaos and whirlwind you are experiencing. Many things that were once taken in stride have now become major hazards in your daily life.

You are in Divorce Country! You never planned to be here, but you are. It's a foreign country with different rules,

regulations, and road signs. It's a place
where your heart is broken and your spirit
is crushed. But *there is hope*!

After twenty-five years of helping
thousands of men and women through the
rapids of divorce, I know that there is hope for you in the
pages of this book. Your spirit can be renewed, and you can
receive the strength and courage to walk through the minefields of Divorce Country.

You can't do it alone! You will need supportive friends
and God's help. I want you to claim this verse from Psalms as
your very own: "The Lord is close to the brokenhearted and
saves those who are crushed in spirit" (34:18, NIV). *You are not
alone in this journey*!

J I M   S M O K E

FAITH

For what is
faith unless it
is to believe
what you do
not see?

SAINT AUGUSTINE

HEALING tHE HURts

He was angry, and his anger was amplified by all the hurt he was experiencing. Finally, he summed up his feelings by blurting out, "Hey, it's pretty simple. Hurt people hurt people."

I thought he was lapsing into some kind of redundancy as I stared at him. Then he said it a second time with a big pause, "Hurt people . . . hurt people." Then I got it.

When we are hurt by someone, we immediately want to hurt them back with some verbal or physical act. We seldom just absorb the hurt, we rarely stop to think and pray about it, and most of us find it difficult to keep moving forward. Instead, we tend to build a monument at our place of pain and spend long periods of mental time thinking of ways to get even.

Divorce can quickly become a war of words and deeds. If you watch the movie *The War of the Roses*, you will know what I mean. When the hurts are deep, the healing is long. Healing only starts when we quit the battle of reprisal and focus all of our energies on the healing process. For most people, healing generally takes two to three years.

Healing can occur when we are in a trusted community of friends. It can also occur when we are alone. When we are alone, we can get in touch with our thinking, feeling, and acting self. It gives us time for reflecting, meditating, and sorting our feelings. It is a good time for journaling, praying, and reading. So many of our human strings are pulled by other people in day-to-day living that being alone can help us collect and sort the fragments of our lives and even make some plans for the future. Being alone allows us to discover who we really are and where we want to go.

Solitary times can also be used to speak with God. We can listen to God and what He is trying to say to us about our healing and growth. Many great leaders in Scripture refused to move in any direction until they were sure they had heard the voice of God.

In solitude, we allow God's quietness, assurance, and peace to wash over us and bring healing to some of the open wounds in our lives. We can tell God how we feel and know that we have been heard.

The prayer for healing hurts in our lives is always the same: Lord, *make me whole*.

BE still
And KNOW
that
I Am God.

PSALM 46:10

Watch Out For the Labels

Our names are labels. They give us a personal identity and connect us to a family of origin.

When a man divorces, his name does not change. When a woman divorces, she may take her maiden name back, retain her former spouse's last name, or remarry and take the last name of her new spouse. Or, as many women are choosing today when they remarry, she can retain her family of origin name and simply put a hyphen between it and her new family name. If a woman did that and remarried several times in her lifetime, she could end up with the name Mary Jones-Smith-Brown-Jackson. That would be grounds for a full-blown identity crisis!

In all seriousness, I have heard some other names given to divorced people that no one would want: *Failure, Victim, Loser, Flake, Stupid, Sinner.* These are the labels we let other people stick on our lives. You could probably add about twenty more here from your own acquired label collection.

Can I suggest some new labels for you today? *Forgiven, Loved, Renewed, Healed, Child of God.*

You did not choose your birth name or the name of the person you married, but you do have a choice with the name that defines who and what you are today.

In the Bible, Jesus saw fit to change Peter's name to "Rock." I am sure that both Peter and the other disciples must have laughed at that new label, but if you read the Book of Acts in the Bible, you soon find that Peter lived up to his new name.

How about you? Is it time to strip away your old labels and inscribe new ones on your life today?

The words of the following hymn talk about God as the great Name Changer for you and I.

> I will change your name.
> You shall no longer be called
> Wounded, outcast, lonely or afraid.
> I will change your name.
> Your new name shall be Confidence,
> joyfulness, overcoming one.
> Faithfulness, friend of God, one
> who seeks my face.

Divorce Divides; God Provides

"Out of work, out of money, and almost out of food and housing."

That's how he described his situation when I asked him how things were going. When I asked how I could help, his pride took over, and he told me he would be fine and that I should not worry about him.

As I watched him walk away, I had serious doubts that he would be fine. He had custody of his two children, and the worry lines on his face were deepening.

Divorce makes life more difficult.

* It is hard to ask for help when you need it . . . and he needed it.

* It is hard to say that you are not making it.

* It is hard to admit that your head and heart are rapidly filling with fear.

* It is hard to wonder how close you are to sleeping in your car and eating at the local mission.

* It is hard to believe that somehow God will take care of all your needs if you will just ask Him and trust that He will.

Divorce is the great divider of life's possessions. It can quickly reduce your economic world to a day-to-day existence. It raises huge questions about personal and family survival. When you lose physical securities, your emotional insecurities surface. Where do you go for help when you need it?

The answer is in two parts. First, I believe that sharing your needs with those closest to you gives others a chance to be a part of your recovery. Try to network with those who are a part of your rebuilding community.

The second part is God. Talk to God. Tell Him your needs, and ask Him to supply them in any manner He chooses. There is a great biblical promise found in Philippians 4:19: "And my God shall supply all your need according to His riches in glory by Christ Jesus." That's a bankable promise that you can wrap your life around.

God will provide for all your needs because He said He would. He loves you that much — so much, in fact, that you can trust Him with the big stuff . . . and the small stuff.

FAith NEVER FAlls ApARt At the AppROAch oF the bouldERs oF liFE. It is wHEN the ROCKs ARE Rolling thAt FAith shows up bEst.

MALCOLM SMITH

A HOME WITH LOVE AT THE CENTER

*J*ack and his two children had just moved from a large home in the suburbs to a two bedroom, one bath apartment on a main thoroughfare. He quickly informed me that he had lost everything that ever meant anything to him. He felt that he and his children would never have a home again.

Jack's feelings are similar to those of many men and women I have met who are traveling through Divorce Country. When a place once called "home" is traded for a temporary living situation in which the people around you are constantly moving in or out, any feelings of stability, longevity, and security last about as long as it takes to unpack. The reality that divorce divides people hits home with a mind-numbing thud.

How do you turn a downsized living space into a love-sized home?

There is a giant difference between a house and a home. Those who live in houses use them as buildings to eat and sleep in and as refuges from the elements. Those who live in homes enjoy them as places where love is reflected not only in interior design and warmth, but even more in the lives of those who live there. Most of us can tell the minute we walk into a dwelling if it is a house or a home.

Real homes breathe life into all who enter, openly welcoming them. It doesn't matter if it's an apartment, a mobile home, or a split-level in the suburbs.

As a kid growing up, I always knew where the houses were and where the homes were. Homes welcomed kids and always seemed to have something for them to eat and drink. You could stay and play, and you never felt like you were in the way.

Divorce may have catapulted you into a less than desirable living situation, but you can choose to make it a house or a home. The stress of a divorce can cause you to think that it just doesn't matter anymore. When that happens, your quality of life deteriorates, and where you live becomes a place just to hang your hat.

No matter where you live or how long you intend to live there, breathe the spirit of love and life into your residence. Looking back on what you may have lost and endlessly grieving that loss will not change your present conditions. The next time you open your front door after a long day at work, say out loud, "I breathe the love of Christ into this dwelling. God, help me make this a true home for me and my family."

Love is something you do!

LiFE FRoM tHE TREEtop

I built a tree house when I was a child. A big, old cherry tree far away from people housed my crude establishment. Whenever life caved in on me or I just needed some valuable quiet, I headed for my tree. I dreamed, I thought, I planned, I pretended, and I ate cherries in season. There are times today when I wish I could run off to my tree house for just a few hours and pretend that life is simple, uncomplicated, and unhurried.

When life aims its heavy artillery at you on all fronts, you need some place to escape to for a time of sifting, sorting, and regrouping. Few people today have such a place, although most wish they had one. As today's world squeezes the essence of real life from us, we desperately need a place of quiet solitude far from the maddening crowd.

Jesus knew the importance of such a place. Before and after major events in His life, He often found a place of rest and refuge away from the pressures of His world.

One of my constant prayers for those going through a divorce is that they would find a place of quiet retreat where

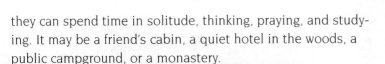

they can spend time in solitude, thinking, praying, and studying. It may be a friend's cabin, a quiet hotel in the woods, a public campground, or a monastery.

Over the years, I have found that a monastery works well for me because it puts me in a spiritual environment while gifting me with peace and quiet. There are hundreds of these around North America as well as in foreign lands.

David tells of the benefits of such a place. In Psalm 31:20 he says, "You shall hide them in the secret place of Your presence from the plots of man; You shall keep them secretly in a pavilion from the strife of tongues."

If God knows we need a hiding place and offers it to us, why are we so hesitant to admit our own need? Too busy, too proud, too important, too what?

Divorce Country is a battle zone most of the time. It is hard to be bombarded daily with its problems without finding restoration in a place of quiet refuge. If you are waiting for someone to grant you permission to head for the trees and build our own tree house, here it is: GO!

Battle zones will always be there, but we can pick and choose our battles as well as our times of escape.

WHERE
rHERE is
pEACE,
God is.

GEORGE HERBERT

Rebounding or Rebuilding?

Remember yo-yos? Not those weirdly shaped plastic models that look like they came from a space movie, but the old-fashioned ones made of hardwood and stamped with the word *DUNCAN* on the side. That simple disk occupied a lot of empty moments in the days of my childhood.

In a moment of frayed nerves and fractured feelings, Joan told me she felt like a yo-yo. She was that spinning orb at the end of the string, and someone else was doing the yanking, pulling, and twirling. Do you ever feel like that?

People are a lot like yo-yos. We can rebound when the string is pulled, but we seldom make any progress rebuilding our lives when someone else is in control.

You cannot move ahead in your life when you are bouncing around at the end of someone else's string. Rebounding must be replaced by rebuilding, and rebuilding requires purposeful planning and responsible goal setting. Rebuilding means taking responsibility for laying out your own game plan and not allowing others to pull your strings.

Do you find yourself spending a lot of time bouncing off the walls while others pull your string? It may be time to sit down with the master builder Jesus and talk to Him about your rebuilding plans.

Writing to some early Christians, Saint Paul said, "Just as you trusted Christ to save you, trust Him too for each day's problems; live in vital union with Him" (Col. 2:6, TLB).

Remember, in a divorce, you get custody of yourself . . . and the yo-yo and the string!

Do not lose your inward peace for anything whatsoever, even if your whole world seems upset.

SAINT FRANCIS
DE SALES

Without risk,
faith is an
impossibility.

SØREN KIERKEGAARD

DON'T SHORT-CIRCUIT YOUR SPIRIT

Circuit breakers are marvelous inventions. If you try to plug too many household appliances into a room of your home, you will trip a switch that throws the entire electrical system in that area off. This can be distracting when you are in a hurry, but it certainly beats burning your house or apartment to the ground.

Wouldn't it be nice if we had the same kind of wiring for our emotions and feelings? When stress and tension build up, we could simply shut down and prevent things like depression, rage, emotional chaos, anxiety, fear, and other assorted ills from becoming too hot.

Divorce can bring any man or woman to the point of emotional overload. Along with our daily list of "to dos," we struggle to fit in all the emotions that zigzag through our mind and spirit. *Craziness* and *insanity* become familiar words that often describe life in the post divorce recovery zone.

How do you keep your mental wiring from overloading and short-circuiting your life?

I believe the **first step** is to take one day at a time, one hour at a time, and one minute at a time. That may sound overly simplistic, but it's a basic principle of all recovery groups. Frame each day, develop a plan to get through it, and don't spend a consummate amount of time worrying about yesterday's agendas. You cannot change yesterday, but you can change today.

In counseling sessions, I listen to many men and women who repeatedly use the line "If I'd only . . ." That mindset can "guilt trip" you into a black hole and prevent you from dealing with the present. Then there are those who spend their time in the land of "What if?" They stack up mountains of fear in their pathway and usually cannot navigate themselves back to the road of recovery.

There is a **second step** that works in close companionship with the first. Each day give the things of that day to the Lord, and He will give you clarity and freedom to walk through whatever lies ahead.

Solomon, the wisest man who ever lived, said, "Commit your works to the Lord, and your thoughts will be established" (Prov. 16:3). Don't let your spirit get short-circuited by all the loose wires in your life!

Say to yourself, *I believe God is in charge*! Then ask yourself, *Is my belief strong enough to let Him take charge*?

GROWTH IS DIGGING IN

We had climbed above the tree line on Mt. Whitney in California. The rest of our journey consisted of rocky switchbacks that finally would put us on top of the highest mountain in the lower forty-eight states. As we rounded a bend, we saw a small, scraggly excuse for a shrub growing right out of a formation of solid rock. Our group stopped long enough to stare and ask, "How could that shrub grow there?"

Years later, we probably are all still wondering how that life could grow in the most unlikely of places. I wonder every day how good can come from bad, how joy can come from sorrow, how victory can come from defeat.

Seeing transformation is one thing; trying to explain it is quite another, which was the case with Andre. He hung behind at the end of a recent seminar. As the crowd dwindled, he came up to me and asked if he could share a thought. He told me that in a weird way, he was thankful for his divorce because it had become his wake-up call in life. It had brought massive changes in his life, and he felt he was finally becoming a strong and growing person. Even the pain of his wife leaving him for another man was being overshadowed by his new growth.

You can grow a great deal in a very unlikely place: Divorce Country. You can be surrounded by enough rocks in Divorce Country to last a lifetime, but out of those sparse surroundings can come new life and growth.

Someone has said that growth is the betrayal of arrangements that were; it is a change that is threatening as well as promising; it is the denial of something and affirmation of something else. Growth is a dangerous and glorious insecurity, but if it's that scary, who needs it? Frankly, you and I need it because if we are not growing, we are dying.

Growth takes strength, and I believe God gives us that strength when we need it. The Bible says, "He gives power to the weak, and to those who have no might He increases strength" (Is. 40:29).

With God's help, that's YOU growing up through the rocks of divorce. You have a choice . . . you can GO through divorce . . . or you can GROW through divorce!

GETTING EVEN WILL NOT GET YOU AHEAD

She was so angry that she wanted to kill someone, specifically her former best friend. I told her that her response would not change the fact that her husband ran off with her best friend.

Somehow she felt the problem was her friend. She thought that if she could remove her friend from the planet, then her husband would return, and they would continue their lives. When I carefully reminded her that people go to prison for killing other people, she unwillingly came back to reality.

You may feel that way today, or you may have felt that way awhile back. Murder may have entered your thoughts in a fleeting moment. We all want to retaliate when an injustice finds its way into our lives. We want to say out loud, "You can't do that to me, and my act of revenge will prove it."

Revenge can be a costly experience. The person seeking revenge is often the person whose life has been forever ruined by someone else's act. Ongoing harassment may be a less violent form of revenge, but it also robs the initiator of emotional energies that can be better used for growth and recovery.

Seeking revenge is a natural human tendency. We learn it in early childhood and spend a lifetime perfecting it. Too often it becomes a way of life that usually destroys relationships and rewards us with a perpetually vindictive spirit.

A vindictive spirit is often a close companion to a blaming spirit. Placing the blame on others is often followed by devious acts of revenge. Our mind says, "They did this or that, and they deserve to be punished for their deed."

When speaking with vengeful people, I have often quoted Saint Paul's letter to the Roman Christians: "'Vengeance is Mine, I will repay,' says the Lord" (Rom. 12:19).

In other words, give your vengeful spirit over to the Lord and let Him take care of the situation. Our problem with that, however, is that God is not in a hurry, and His vengeance may be years away.

Don't waste valuable time plotting acts of revenge on other people even if you feel they deserve it. Why should you give *them* the time you need for *your* own personal growth?

Remember, every time you engage in a vengeful act, you give a little of yourself away. You are too valuable to do that!

A life of reaction is a life of slavery. One must fight for a life of action, not reaction.

RITA MAE BROWN

THINKING IT OVER... AND OVER AND OVER!

Do you ever find yourself wide-awake and staring at the bedroom ceiling at 4 A.M.? Your mind is racing like mad while your body screams for rest. In the dark of the night, past events in your life collide with present realities, and you are left with the question we all wrestle with from time to time: "Why me, Lord?"

We all write scripts for our lives. Perhaps we have seen too many movies, but we always want a happy ending to our stories. The proposed script for marriage is to live happily ever after. Our script for our children is that they might grow up healthy and wise and that they might find success in their own lives and help convince the world that we were good parents.

A seminar participant recently summed up her condition in life for me by stating, "Somebody stole my happy ending from my life, and I want it back!" Most of the people I work with would echo her plea and add an additional one: "Why did this happen to me, and what did I do wrong?"

There are some things in this life that will always lie about two short steps beyond our understanding. What we cannot solve we can only accept, and then we must move on in our journey. If we really believe that God is in charge and is directing our steps each day, then we can leave the unanswered questions to His care and wisdom. I sometimes believe that the reason Christians will spend eternity with the Lord is that it will take that long for God to answer all the questions they brought along from this life. King Solomon said, "Since the Lord is directing our steps, why try to understand everything that happens along the way?" (Prov. 20:24, TLB).

If we commit our steps to the Lord and believe that He is Lord of both the sensible and the nonsensible things in our life, we will find some release from those 4 A.M. Maalox moments in our lives.

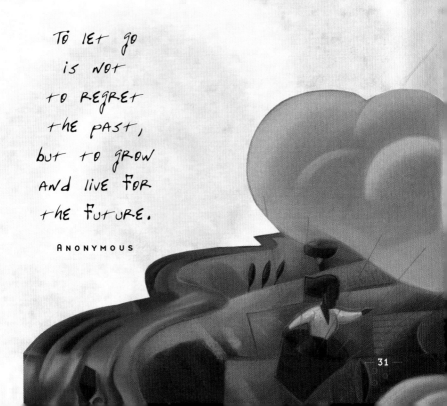

To let go
is not
to regret
the past,
but to grow
and live for
the future.

ANONYMOUS

31

You may
trust the Lord
too little,
but you can
never trust
Him too much.

Anonymous

GOD AND MR. CLEAN

Remember Mr. Clean? In the commercials, he would come into a house and perform his great cleaning act. No matter how terrible the mess or how deep the scum, Mr. Clean could make it all bright and shiny. Just like new.

Most of us have a shelf or cabinet filled with every cleaning compound ever invented. With these, we can take spots out of everything. If it's not clean, we have the stuff to make it clean.

Wouldn't it be great if you could buy an Emotional Cleaning Compound? Or a Feelings Detergent? Or a Bad-Spot-in-Your-Life Remover? In the real world of everyday struggles and questions, there is no magical Mr. Clean that can make everything right again in your life.

A long time ago, Job learned a simple yet profound truth. In the concluding chapter of Job's struggles, he finally made a statement that you and I should never forget: "God can do everything!" (paraphrase of Job 42:2). God challenged Job until Job must have finally given in and said, "Okay, okay. I got the message! You can do everything!"

Have YOU gotten the message yet? Or are you still arguing with God over the small points? Do you believe God can help you rebuild your life and the lives of your family members post divorce? Do you believe God will supply your daily needs? Do you believe that God can protect you from harm? Do you believe God can help you start a new career? Build new friendships? Dream new dreams?

Last week I conducted a second marriage ceremony for two people from one of our singles groups. As I watched them exchange their marriage vows, they radiated happiness, and my mind went back a few years to the tears, pain, and anguish the woman was experiencing as she went through a divorce. Hope for a happy future wasn't even a dim light at the end of her tunnel. How different her future turned out!

With God's help, she is now at a place of new beginnings. Yes, God can do everything! He can do everything for you!

DON'T WORRY,
BE HAPPY!

The song had a simple message to it . . . "Don't worry, be happy." It was imprinted on t-shirts, buttons, bumper stickers . . . and human memories. We hummed it, sang it, and hoped it would take all our worries away. Years later we find our happiness still tainted by our cumulative list of daily worries.

The woods in Divorce Country are full of worries. Will I have enough money to survive? Will I survive? Will my children survive? Where will we live? What if we end up on the street?

Worries have a way of numbing our mind and spirit and robbing us of our joy, our hope, and our future. The more we worry, the greater our obstacles become, and the less equipped we are to climb over them.

A wise person once said that 90 percent of the things we worry about never happen. If that is true, then we waste a lot of time worrying. But we will never live totally free of worry. A degree of it comes with just being human.

Worry is best resolved when replaced with trust and action. When I take action steps on the things that swirl endlessly through my mind, there is no need to worry. I believe one of the best action steps is to turn all our worries over to God. One of my favorite verses of Scripture says, "Be anxious for nothing, but in everything by prayer and supplication, with thanksgiving, let your requests be made known to God; and the peace of God, which surpasses all understanding, will guard your hearts and minds through Christ Jesus" (Phil. 4:6-7).

The formula for "Don't worry, be happy" lies in this Scripture. TELL GOD EVERYTHING! Don't leave out any of the details. Cover the waterfront! Give Him the whole ten yards! Don't hold anything back!

Once you have done that, God promises that His peace will surround you and will guard your heart. And when His peace flows through you, you will be happy!

Our problem is that our problems become our worries, and our unresolved worries derail our daily happiness. When we give those worries over to God, they become His to resolve and not ours.

I talked with a woman recently whose legal issues in her divorce were worrying her into a state of near collapse. I suggested that she talk with an attorney who is a friend of mine to find some resolution. Several days later she called to say that my friend had helped her solve many of her legal problems and she was relieved and free from worry again.

Don't waste 90 percent of your life worrying. Tell God everything and find people who can give you practical help.

DON'T BLAME GOD FOR HIS CHILDREN'S MISTAKES

We bumped into each other at the mall. He had attended a recent divorce recovery workshop of mine, and I asked him how he was doing. His response was, "Great everywhere but in church."

When I asked for further explanation, he mentioned that all of his friends and acquaintances in his church did their very best to avoid speaking to him on Sunday. He felt very alone and rejected and said, half smiling, "I feel like I'm wearing the wrong deodorant."

You may identify with this man because his story is shared by hundreds of thousands of other single-again men and women in churches of all faiths across North America. It is a tragic commentary on people who are supposed to share the love of God with everyone, regardless of whether they understand or agree with their struggle.

Divorce is the only major life crisis in which most of your social support systems disappear, and many new support systems are only temporary.

I struggle with trying to understand church people who cannot rally around a person who is experiencing divorce. I know it is hard to remain neutral and caring if they have been a friend to both the husband and wife, but I also know that real friends don't bail out on you when you are faced with one of life's most difficult struggles.

What can you do if your church family offers no love or care while your world is falling apart? Here are a couple of solutions that work well.

* Don't get mad at God. He didn't do it.

* Don't get mad at His children. They should know better, but they are human.

* Don't abandon your personal walk with God. You need Him.

* If you don't feel loved and cared for in your church, find a new one.

Divorce can make you mad at everyone, including God. You may have even prayed that God would intervene and put your marriage back together. But it hasn't happened, and your faith in God may be a little thin right now. It may be hard to really believe God loves you when He doesn't give you what you have asked for.

Many divorced people that I meet have been forced to live out a bad decision made by their former spouse. That bad decision has placed them where they do not want to be, but God's promise to you from Hebrews 13:5 is still in effect: "I will never leave you nor forsake you."

Reminder: God loves divorced people. He just hates divorce because He knows it hurts His children.

God plus you is always a majority!

To Forgive Is to Live

My part of the seminar had ended, and we were preparing for the group discussion time when I saw him. He was red-faced and fuming, and heading in my direction. Since I dislike confrontation, I looked for an escape route. None available. Confrontation inevitable.

In a machine-gun burst of words, he informed me that I was delusional if I believed he should someday ask his former spouse to forgive him for the things that he did to contribute to the failure of their marriage. He further informed me that the break-up was his wife's fault, and thinking about forgiveness was totally ridiculous. (He actually used another word here that I cannot use in this book.)

After some additional unkind comments, he stormed out of the room and went straight to his car. I did not expect him to return to the workshop before its conclusion.

The next week, during our open sharing time, he reappeared and raised his hand to speak. I wondered if I should make a hasty retreat or acknowledge him. As I nodded in his direction, he began to tell the group a story. He said, "I left here last week angry and upset, determined not to ever return. The next night I was shopping at the supermarket, and I almost ran into my former spouse when I came around an aisle. I looked at her and said, 'Will you forgive me for the things that, knowingly and unknowingly, I did to contribute to the failure of our marriage?' The words were out of my mouth before I even knew I was saying them. She looked at me and said, 'Yes. Will you do the same for me?' I cannot describe what happened at that moment, other than an incredible load was lifted from my life and a new spirit washed over me. The horrible battles we had been having disappeared, and I felt free and renewed."

He looked at me and said, "Did you brainwash me or hypnotize me last week?"

I said, "No, but I think maybe God did."

For the remainder of the workshop, the change in him was striking. Does that sound weird to you? It shouldn't because the need for forgiveness is emphasized in the Bible. In the middle of the Lord's Prayer, I read these words: "And forgive us our debts, as we forgive our debtors."

Forgiveness is God's detergent to help wash the garbage out of our lives and allow us to live responsibly in relationships with one another. You can't live if you can't forgive.

You may not feel like forgiving today. It may be a long way off for you, but please file this page for future reference.

PlEASE! JUSt A LittlE PEACE ANd QuiEt!

The sign at the entrance of my favorite monastery says it all: "No Hunting Except For Peace." Every time I drive past it, I am reminded that my hours there are to be peaceful and that my flagging spirit will be renewed. There are times when I wish I could take up permanent residence there forever and leave the turbulence of the outside world behind. When I leave and drive through those monastery gates, I wonder if a departing sign should read, "Good-bye Peace. Hello Chaos!"

When Ruth came in for her appointment, she looked like the world had rolled over her and left its imprint on her face. Her story was about a pain-filled marriage marred by emotional and physical abuse. After twenty years, she finally left her husband using the minimal energy she could pull together to save her own life. She kept saying, "I want to go somewhere where it's peaceful and quiet and rest for a long time."

I recommended several places to her, one being my peaceful monastery out near the desert. I knew that she was just a short step away from a mental hospital and desperately needed a big dose of peace and quiet.

Going to a peaceful place when we need it is a wonderful gift. When that's not immediately possible, there is another alternative: Go to God and ask Him to surround your situation, your struggle, and your person with His peace.

What is the difference between God's peace and our peace? I believe ours is conditional while God's is supernatural. Ours is influenced by life situations, but God's peace can be present despite our life situations.

Divorce can rob your peace. It can cause you to wonder if you will ever have another peaceful moment as long as you live. The good news is that God can bring His peace into any situation that you are experiencing. Remember this verse: "May the Lord of peace himself give you his peace no matter what happens" (2 Thess. 3:16, TLB).

That's a tall order because it has no exception clause. It is inclusive because it says, "NO MATTER WHAT HAPPENS."

I believe real peace is not just the absence of exterior noise. I believe it is the real presence of Jesus, the Prince of Peace, radiating from inside of you and passing through you to the life situations that swirl around you. This could be described as learning to live "inside out." Let the peace you know on the inside control your response to any and all events that happen outside of you.

You may need to find a place of peace to retreat to periodically, whether it's a physical place or inside your heart. God's peace is with you no matter where you go. He gives His peace when we ask Him for it!

A Light At the End of the Tunnel

I am not claustrophobic, but I always have an eerie feeling when I start driving through a tunnel. I wonder what would happen to me if my car broke down in the middle of the tunnel, if the tunnel fell down on the middle of my car, or if the tunnel had no end and I was stuck in there forever. I always press a little harder on the accelerator when I see the light at the end of the tunnel.

We have several choices when we confront the emotional mountains in our lives. We can climb over them, travel around them, or *tunnel through them*. Whatever we choose, it is always hard work, and it takes time and energy. The ultimate goal is always the same: move beyond the mountain.

You probably could list numerous mountains you are now facing in Divorce Country. Financial, relational, emotional, spiritual, and familial are only a few. Your greatest danger is that any mountain could block your growth permanently and immobilize you in your journey toward wholeness and healing.

All mountains are conquered slowly. In his famous Possibility Thinkers Creed, Dr. Robert Schuller says, "Lord, when

I face a mountain, do not let me quit! Give me the strength to keep on striving until I climb over, find a pass through, or tunnel underneath. And if my best efforts fail, give me the patience to stay and the perception to see the possibilities of turning my mountain into a gold mine with your help."

Saint Paul asks a simple question in Romans 8:31: "If God is for us, who can be against us?" Your answer might be "Everyone and everything seems to be against me." If that is the way you feel, remember that God is for you. He loves you, and with His help, all the mountains in your pathway can be conquered.

HOPE

HOPE NEVER
SPREAD HER
golden wings
but in
unFathomable
seas.

RALPH WALDO
EMERSON

Windows of Hope

I start every divorce recovery workshop by asking members of the audience to share something good or something bad from their week. In a recent workshop, a woman stood and shared that her husband had left her after thirty-five years of marriage, just five months short of their planned retirement. Their retirement cabin was about to be sold along with their primary residence. She feared she would have to find a job and go to work, but she did not know if her health would hold up. She summed up her thoughts by saying, "All my hopes have been dashed, and there is nothing ahead for me now!"

Does that sound like a familiar story? The increase of divorce in long-term marriages is climbing dramatically today. Future plans and goals go out the window when divorce papers are signed. Hope often follows close behind.

Having hope is living with the expectancy that good things will happen tomorrow even though it doesn't seem that way today. Many times our hopes are hinged on other people, events, finances, and so on. When those hopes don't materialize, we feel betrayed and in despair.

There is an old saying that helps put hope into a realistic light: "If it's going to be, it's up to me!" This means that I am responsible for attaining my hopes. If I give that responsibility to someone else, I can be endlessly disappointed.

King David saw both victories and defeats in his life. In Psalm 71:14 he said, "But I will hope continually, and will praise You yet more and more." David proclaimed that he would always make two things a priority . . . hope and praise to the Lord. He claimed those two things as his sole and personal responsibility. No one else could do them for him.

Divorce can dash your hopes on the rocks of reality, but it can only take your hope away if YOU allow it to happen. With the help of God, will you open a new window of hope in your life today?

Hope is
an adventure,
a going
forward,
a confident
search for a
rewarding life.

DR. KARL
MENNINGER

BUT I DON'T WANT TO LET GO!

Letting go of a relationship that was once the most meaningful relationship in your life is usually a long slow process that does not happen overnight. The struggle to let go is waged on three basic fronts: the emotional, the relational, and the practical. All three take tremendous energy and time.

A man in our workshop summed up his attempt at letting go with these words: "I keep letting go and letting go and letting go. When will I finally let go of letting go?" Does that sound familiar?

Letting go begins when you decide to quit hanging on to a relationship that no longer exists. Your mind, heart, and spirit may tell you to hang on and believe in the possibility of restoring your marriage. But reality may be telling you that the door has long since been closed, and it's time to move on with your life!

I have watched thousands of people struggle with this decision over the years. It may well be the toughest one to face in Divorce Country.

I remember a lady in one of our seminars who tossed her wedding ring at me after I said, "When it's time to let go, LET GO!" When I picked up the ring and asked who had lost it, she stood and said, "I did . . . finally. And I don't want it back."

She informed our audience that she had been divorced for four years. Her husband had remarried and had moved to another city. He even had a new child. She had convinced herself that as long as she wore her wedding ring, the marriage wasn't really over. But in that moment of ring tossing, she finally let go and began a new journey.

Moving on and letting go are positive steps toward rebuilding your life. Too many divorced people tend to live in a holding pattern so that they will not have to face the mental and emotional termination of their marriage.

Moving on is closing old doors. You can't leave them ajar to see if your former spouse might squeeze through again at some future date. When the possibility of restoration is gone, bringing closure to that relationship is the key to new beginnings.

Do you remember that old slogan, "Let go and let God"? The best way to let go of things already gone is to commit the unknown to God and trust Him with your future. As long as you hang on to a dead relationship, God cannot give you a new sense of direction and lead you to where He wants you to go.

In his letter to the Philippians, Saint Paul offers some good advice: "Forgetting those things which are behind and reaching forward to those things that are ahead, I press toward the goal for the prize of the upward call of God in Christ Jesus" (Phil. 3:13).

Are you up to speed in the "letting go" department?

Living At the Crossroads

We had talked for almost an hour about the forthcoming changes in Sam's life. The more we talked, the more confused he seemed to be. He told me that he wanted everything back the way it once was. I reminded him that he could not go back, and I encouraged him to make some choices and get on with his life.

Sam may be a little like you . . . like all of us. We become fearful that we will make the wrong choice, but we also are fearful if we make the right choice. We would rather not choose at all or would prefer to let someone else choose for us.

Our choices often create dramatic changes in our lives and in the lives of those around us. The many threads of those changes can weave through our lives for years to come.

Divorce is a critical turning point that can bring about both negative and positive changes. It can quickly change your priorities in life. Things you once deemed important can quickly be replaced by what you have learned is REALLY IMPORTANT.

A divorce can strengthen or weaken your faith and belief system. The pain of divorce can remind you of your humanity

and can bring you face-to-face with the reality that we are all wounded healers.

You, and only you, can make the decisions that will have either a positive or negative influence on the rest of your life. I watch many divorced men and women who decide to live in a holding pattern until the "right someone" comes along to help them make the right choices and right changes. But in doing so, they wait a long time only to discover that the "right person" can make the wrong choices.

Remember, in a divorce, you get custody of yourself. That custody puts you and you alone in charge of the decision to make changes in your life and to live them out with hope and confidence.

You may be at a crossroads right now, but remember that you have the great promise from Isaiah 42:16 that says, "I will make darkness light before them, and crooked places straight. These things I will do for them, and not forsake them."

People decide to change when the pain of the situation is almost equal to the fear of the change. Then the risk is taken.

ANONYMOUS

HOW TO MAKE THE Impossible Possible

His words rang in my ears long after the meeting ended. "You don't have a problem. You have a possibility!" I was irritated with this leader because I had clearly defined what I thought was a problem only to be told it was some kind of golden opportunity that had landed on the front steps of my life.

Many years later, I now understand what this leader was saying. It is how you view any situation that determines its eventual outcome.

Are you a possibility thinker? Do you look at your daily list of challenges and respond by saying, "can do" or "can't do"? Is your battle cry, "This problem can't be resolved"?

If you took a minute right now and listed all the things in your life that would fall under the category of "impossible problems," how long would your list be? If you made a second list under the title "possible solutions," how long would that list be?

Some of the "impossibles" I have heard from formerly married men and women include:

* I will never ever marry again.
* I will never trust anyone again.
* Since my marriage failed, I will always be a failure.
* My children will probably get divorced someday.
* I will now be miserable until I die.
* I will never be happy again.

Many who have said those things have lived through their divorce only to find out that none of them are true.

With God's help, mistaken beliefs can fade away. Jesus explained many spiritual truths to His small band of disciples. For instance, in Matthew 19:25, the disciples asked, "Who then can be saved?" Jesus' answer was simple: "With men this is impossible, but with God all things are possible."

Jesus' incredible statement not only related to the disciples, but it also includes you and I when we are faced with impossibilities. There are no impossibilities where God is concerned.

Sometimes it is a quantum leap from the impossible to the possible. Only God can help you navigate the space between the two.

Living in the Quiet Zone

Susan was fit to be tied. She had just gone through another grueling forty-minute telephone discussion with her former spouse. What started out as an attempt to resolve some visitation times for the children quickly escalated to a full-blown yelling, accusing, and crying match. Debris from the past hurled over the telephone lines and exploded on each party with the impact of a grenade.

Susan finally looked at me and said, "I can't live this way anymore. The divorce was bad enough, but these aftereffects are even worse. What can I do?"

I shared with her the two questions I have asked many people caught in the divorce crossfire. What can I live with? What can I not live with? These questions help people set up protective boundaries. They also help establish priorities.

You can waste a lot of time and energy fighting battles that have no meaningful solution. If you take the time to get out of the battle zone, you can begin to focus on your own growth and development. When the land mines of potential conflict over long-dead issues are placed in your pathway,

stop long enough to say out loud, "I refuse to use my mental and emotional energies in this conflict. I will focus on my desire to live a quiet life, I will mind my own business, and I will get on with the real work of my life."

Someone once summed up useless conflict by stating, "Put the past in the past and learn to live in the present." Rehashing yesterday's mistakes will not make living in today any easier. Continuous aggravation does not make for a quiet spirit.

Your number one priority after divorce is rebuilding your family and yourself. You can only do that if you stay away from yesterday's garbage, and you'll need intent and determination to guide you through it.

Proverbs 15:1 is a great aid to growth and is worth memorizing: "A soft answer turns away wrath, but a harsh word stirs up anger."

The words of Saint Paul also are helpful: "But we urge you, brethren, that you increase more and more; that you also aspire to lead a quiet life, to mind your own business, and to work with your own hands, as we commanded you" (1 Thess. 4:10-11).

If you are constantly in the battle zone, then relocate to the quiet zone.

> Action springs not from thought, but from a readiness for responsibility.
>
> DIETRICH BONHOEFFER

NEW BEGINNINGS...
PERMISSION GRANTED

It happened on a day when I wished I had more anonymity in my life. My wife and I were leaving an area restaurant when a woman yelled my name from the very far side of the establishment. Everyone started looking around to see whom she was calling. Before we could even pay our bill and sneak away, she came running toward us.

When she was within speaking distance, she asked the question that usually embarasses both of us: "Hi, remember me?"

I did my usual "mumble stumble" and said, "Vaguely." (That means "No.")

She told me her name and said she was in one of my workshops a few years back. Then she thanked me for all my help and proceeded to share her journey of growth with me.

When she came into our workshop, she felt defeated, demoralized, and was in great despair. She had no job to support herself and felt she had no future. She explained that my weekly emphasis on new beginnings slowly began to sink into her head and heart. By the time the workshop was over, she was filled with optimism and hope.

She went to a real estate school and became a successful realtor. She then opened her own office, hired a few other men and women who were also climbing the ladder of vocational growth, and charged full speed ahead using her many sales gifts. She soon purchased her own home, and because of her extensive traveling, she was thinking about getting her MBA degree.

She literally bubbled as she talked. As I walked to my car, I wanted to punch the air with my fist and yell, "All right!" One more person had lifted herself out of the mire!

Injecting people with new hope is a vital part of recovery. Someone needs to yell in your ear, "You can do it!" When you find out that you can do it, you have the same sensation you had when you first rode your bike without the training wheels or someone hanging on to you . . . EXHILARATION!

If you are looking for permission to do the difficult and almost impossible, here it is . . . PERMISSION GRANTED! GO FOR IT!

The future is called 'perhaps' which is the only possible thing to call the future. And the important thing is not to allow that to scare you.

TENNESSEE WILLIAMS

REACH UP
AS FAR AS
YOU CAN,
AND GOD WILL
REACH DOWN
ALL THE WAY.

JOHN H. VINCENT

LESSONS FROM THE LITTLE ENGINE

Once in a while I spend some time in the children's section of our local bookstore. I wander around and look at books written for children that adults need to read. I recently bought *The Little Engine That Could*. I remembered it from my childhood and decided it needed to become a part of my adulthood. A few nights after I purchased it, I read it to my divorce recovery class, and I am sure they thought I had flipped out.

Two lines from the book struck me as very important. The first one is what the little engine says to get moving: "I think I can, I think I can, I think I can." The second is a reflective thought after the little engine accomplishes its task: "I thought I could, I thought I could, I thought I could." Between those two lines lies the heroic story of a little engine that successfully accomplished what others chose not to even attempt.

Little children start out in life thinking they can do anything. Then they become adults who think they can do only some things. Then when they fail, they often wind up thinking they can't do anything. This is when we need little engines that teach us lessons of hope in pulling our train through life.

Your divorce may have run you right off the tracks in life, and you're left wondering if any kind of engine can get you moving over the mountains again. Faith that climbs mountains will come when you believe that God's power and your desire can get you moving again. God's help for you today comes from Philippians 4:13: "I can do all things through Christ who strengthens me."

When we hook up to God's power, we not only will be on the right track, but we will have the pulling power each day to climb the mountains of fear, loneliness, depression, rejection, and loss.

Run out and buy your own copy of *The Little Engine That Could*. You can learn some big lessons from that little engine.

Avoid Emotional Collisions

The man on the phone had a simple question: "If I come to your six week divorce recovery workshop, will I meet a woman to date?"

I asked him how long he had been divorced, and he told me two months. As our conversation continued, I tried to tell him that he needed recovery and growth far more than he needed a date. There was a dead silence on the phone when I told him that it usually takes one to two years before someone is really ready to start dating or thinking about a new relationship.

I doubt that he ever made it to our workshop. His priority was finding someone, not finding himself.

I have discovered that many men and women don't want to endure the healing process alone after a divorce. They would rather shift some of their load to someone else or even remarry as quickly as possible. When that happens, I describe it as an emotional collision. After many years of working in this area, I have found that most emotional collisions only lead to wrecked lives, emotional disasters, and second divorces.

Personal pain makes us very vulnerable. Too many people feel that their pain will go away if they can just find someone to share it with.

Nadine felt just that way. Several months after she went through our seminar, she found herself in a rapidly heating up relationship that led to marriage after only a few months of dating. She claimed to be the exception to the rule — she didn't think she needed one to two years of transition. Today she is the victim of a second divorce after only eighteen short months of marriage. She now says she will wait five years before she begins another relationship.

Becoming whole takes time. It involves learning from where you have been and looking to the future. No one can speed up your recovery process. You cannot microwave your growth and healing. Divorce is not a headache relieved by two aspirin. It is a life ache that heals slowly but surely if you do your homework and give it time.

Long-term growth requires patience and good direction. Yes, there will be a time to build new relationships and consider remarriage, but not in just a few months after your divorce is finalized. Remember these three words: **avoid emotional collisions.**

Is There a Butterfly Stuck in Your Cocoon?

The poster showed a beautiful multi-colored butterfly. The message printed on it said, "You can fly, but that cocoon has to go." I bought it and put it up on my office wall for the next year. Many of the people I was working with at the time needed to hear the message so that they could slowly learn how to fly again.

You may feel a reasonable degree of safety when you stay in your cocoon. The protective walls can keep you from injury. The immobile cocoon is nonthreatening to anyone in the immediate area, and there is little danger of falling when you are not flying.

Divorce can be compared to many things. It can be a battlefield and a cocoon of safety all in the same day. It can be one glorious excuse for not moving ahead in your life while blaming a former spouse for your indefinite immobilization. Those who safely hug their cocoon to themselves will only view life from the ground level. Those who choose to fly will be able to see from that all-encompassing aerial view, and they will experience the thrill of seeing where their wings can take them.

Are you firmly stuck in your divorce cocoon, or have you begun to gently try your new wings? When you choose to grow *through* your divorce, you also should choose to live *beyond* divorce. You can make better progress when flying than you can when walking or crawling, but the divorce cocoon has to be shed.

I meet people who are trying to fly while they hang on to their cocoon. It doesn't work. That cocoon has to go!

When you are divorcing or are newly divorced, you will need a protective cocoon for a while. But you don't want to hide there for the rest of your life.

Your promise for today is found in Isaiah 40:31: "They shall mount up with wings like eagles."

Is there a beautiful butterfly stuck in your cocoon today just waiting to spread its wings and fly into new adventures?

MAKING PLANS, MOVING AHEAD

The sign was right on target. It said, "Shoot at nothing and that is exactly what you will hit." It reminded me of a recent conversation I had with a lady in her sixties who was coming out of a long and hard divorce battle. I asked her what her plans were for the future. She sadly echoed the words I hear from many divorced people, "What future? My life is over now, and I will just keep existing until I die." I wanted to yell loudly that her life was still moving and that she had to make new plans to replace the old ones.

Divorce ruins the plans that people make. It ruins family plans, business plans, vocational plans, retirement plans, and educational plans. It moves people from definitive plans to "maybe someday" plans. A once organized life can become unorganized chaos. Your prayer can easily become, "Dear God, find me someone who has an organized plan for my life. Today! Amen."

During a divorce, many human plans run into a detour or are put on hold. Some are forever abandoned, and no new ones take their place.

Living without plans can mean living without a purpose. When your life has no purpose, it will lose its meaning.

The Bible encourages us to make plans with God's help and ask God to direct us in the fulfilling of those plans (Prov. 3:6). He only asks one simple thing: that we put Him first in all our plans. This may be simple for you or very difficult. Many people want to put themselves first and God second. As a result, their plans may not succeed.

I often ask people in our workshops to share three plans they have made for the next year. Some jokingly respond by saying, "Keep breathing." Others have really set some goals and are happy to share them as they work toward them. We put ourselves on the line anytime we share our goals with others because they can hold us accountable from time to time by asking how we are doing.

Are you hoping someone will come along with a set of goals for you? Or are you setting your own goals with the Lord's help and guidance?

No one other than you and God should be entrusted with making plans for your life.

The most effective way to ensure the value of the future is to confront the present courageously and constructively.

ROLLOW MAY

You can
never plan
the future
by the
past.

EDMUND BURKE

Is There Life After Divorce?

Divorce can often be compared to an auto demolition derby. When I was younger, we would attend stock car races where we knew the last event was the demolition derby. Everyone anxiously waited for twenty-five cars to smash each other into oblivion as the noise levels climbed higher and higher. The last car still running took the monetary prize for the evening. Then everyone went home, knowing that the cars probably would be scraped into piles of twisted metal and escaping fumes.

Divorce can often be compared to a demolition derby. The playing field starts out with two people running into each other, causing major damage. The contest then continues with someone trying to survive even though the majority will become immobilized and will be left in ruin. When the competition is over, it takes a long time . . . sometimes a lifetime . . . to clean up all the debris. I am not sure that there is always a winner. Most of the time, everyone loses something.

Sometimes the debris of a divorce appears in tangible form. It can run the gamut from frequent clashes with a former spouse to the entanglements of child raising, establishing a new career, or striving to contend with economic realities.

At the tangible level, the debris clogs your brain in the quiet hours of the night when the mind needs to unwind. Questions surface about your tomorrows and whether you will ever again share them with a special someone. Should you go it alone and travel light through the rest of your life? Should you keep looking around palm trees and pillars for a great possibility to walk into your life? Should you join a video or computer dating service and venture into the world of techno dating? Or is it wiser and safer just being who you are and staying single again?

The world of the single-again man or woman is a world of putting the past behind you, cleaning up the wreckage your divorce has brought into your life, and taking a long look over the edge of tomorrow.

It is trusting God with your future while inviting Him to direct your conscious thoughts and plans. But remember: God has given you a mind to use. He does not expect you to become some kind of spiritual robot who never thinks and only acts when commanded by God.

Your future can be your friend, and you can move creatively and constructively toward it by formulating your goals and objectives a little each day. I like the promise found in Psalm 37:5: "Commit your way to the Lord, trust also in Him, and He shall bring it to pass." Remember, God wrote the book about fresh starts and new beginnings!

TOO MANY DECISIONS, TOO LITTLE TIME

Have you ever wished you were a lot smarter than you are? Have you ever wished you had the business savvy of Donald Trump, the negotiating skills of Henry Kissinger, the charm of Prince Charming, or the wisdom of King Solomon?

We all spend some of our time around the Wisdom Wishing Well. One of our greatest fears in life is that we will make the wrong decisions. Some people avoid that fear by making no decisions at all.

When I met him, Steven was peering over the edge of the Well. His questions came at me with machine gun speed. Should I move? Should I change careers? Should I buy or rent a place to live? Should I accept my parents' offer to move in with them? Should I try to get sole custody of my children?

I finally had to put my hands up in front of him to stop the questions. I knew his struggle well as he began a long and tentative journey through Divorce Country. He wanted to make all the right decisions, and he wanted to make them all in sixty seconds. . . . and he wanted me to tell him what to do with each decision.

For most men and women, the landscape of divorce is littered with more questions than answers. It takes time, patience, thinking, and praying to come up with the wisest and best answers. It also requires risk.

Making decisions calls for more than knee-jerking our way through tough issues. It involves a willingness to do research and homework. It means collecting wisdom from those who have been down the same road. It also requires that we bring the questions to God and wait patiently for Him to show us the answers.

We all live in an age of impatience and uncertainty. The age of security and guarantees is long past. We want to microwave our answers just like our food. We live in a world where processes are denied and instant resolutions are expected.

I find it increasingly more difficult to get participants to attend all six weeks of our recovery workshop and read the textbook while they are doing it. Everyone wants the shortest route to an answer and the quickest antidote to their pain.

Reflect for a few minutes on the Scripture found in the Book of James: "If any of you lacks wisdom, let him ask of God, who gives to all liberally and without reproach, and it will be given to him" (1:5). I believe this is the best starting point when you are confronted with decisions.

A lack of decision-making can cause you to live your life in a holding pattern and rob you of the freedom to move your life ahead. The decisions you make today are the building blocks and foundation for all your tomorrows!

FROM TEARS
to Joy

I heard an important comment recently in a divorce support group. A woman had apparently been listening to a sad story coming from the man in her group. Finally, she looked directly at him and said, "Why don't you just go and have a good cry! You'll feel better!"

As I walked away, I smiled to myself. I have heard many women say that, including my own mother. But I have yet to hear one man say that to another. We all know men are forbidden to cry or even to suggest that anyone else should cry. Besides, crying does horrible things to your face. You have trouble seeing clearly while crying, and your nose and eyes leak in unison.

When was the last time you had a good, long, really cascading cry? How did you feel at the end of it? Better? Worse? Soggy?

I believe tears are a gift from God. They allow us to express emotions that we cannot adequately put into words. Tears also have a way of drawing people close to each other. Tears speak when words won't come through our lips. Tears

are for big people and little people. Tears are for all people because we all cry in the same language.

It is hard to think of divorce as a time for sowing anything. Some refer to it as the great stagnation. Yet, during the process and recovery, we are planting seeds of new growth through our tears. It is hard to believe that somewhere beyond our tears there will be joy once again, but Psalm 126:5 says, "Those who sow in tears shall reap in joy." I cannot make that promise to you, but God can — and has — made it.

When I talk to people about the divorce recovery process, some of them only want to know one thing: "When will I quit crying?" The answer might be, "When it is time to quit sowing."

Seeds of recovery need fertile growing conditions. It's okay to water your seeds!

TEARS ARE
the UNSPOKEN
WORDS dAMMED
up behiNd
the RIVER
of ouR liFE.

WHEN IT'S TIME FOR CLOSURE

There are three words every child hears frequently: "Close the door." Children specialize in leaving the front door wide open. Parents spend years trying to explain the purpose of doors to children. Then, as adults, we discover that some doors don't close very easily. The mental and emotional doors we pass through in life often have pretty rusty hinges.

Closing doors is hard in Divorce Country. We are forced to acknowledge our history. We also have to file our memories, process our healing, and keep moving ahead while frequently looking back over our shoulders.

There is a place in every closure process for erecting some kind of growth marker or point of passage. It is a way of saying, "I have been there, passed on, and am not going back." Closure often needs symbols or seals to make it final. Each person must decide how to close and seal the doors to yesterday.

Closure would be easy if you could put all the remnants of a former life in boxes and stack them in your garage. The real struggle is to contain the filing cabinets in your mind and keep them from spilling their contents back into your life each day.

God's help is always present when we must close the doors to yesterday in our lives. He assures us that if we deal honestly and humbly with our places of closure, He will teach us the best way to put seals on the doors.

What acts have you initiated to finally close old doors in your life and move toward the possibility of opening new ones? In the land beyond divorce, some doors just close by them-selves, but some doors must be closed by you — an important step if you are to move your life ahead.

Acts of closure are seldom easy. They are the signposts that mark our lives and tell us where we have been and where we are headed.

Custody of Whom?

She came into my office excited and yelling, "It's finally over!" She was waving her divorce papers like they were the liberation flag of an imprisoned person finally set free from some distant tyrannical nation.

We talked and joked as she celebrated her victory after a four-year battle over money, possessions, and alcohol. As she was about to leave, she also loudly stated, "I got custody of my children, too." I couldn't resist telling her what I have told thousands of other divorced people over the years: "Mary, don't forget: you also got custody of yourself!" She then thanked me for spoiling her celebration and headed down the hall.

It's true. Along with the myriad responsibilities you have after a divorce, you also get custody of yourself, even though no divorce papers state that fact. Taking custody of yourself can be both exciting and scary at the same moment. It reinforces the fact that you are now a majority of one again, and there will be no spouse around to design and help remodel the rest of your life.

It takes real strength and tremendous inner resources, along with a strong cheerleading squad of friends, to take complete and personal custody of yourself. I believe it also takes the strong hand of God in your life.

God packs gifts, talents, and abilities into every person He creates. We have a personal choice: we can use what we are given, or we can leave our giftedness undiscovered and unused for a lifetime.

What do you want to do with the rest of your life? What personal gifts are you ready to finally unwrap and put to good use?

A man who lived for years in a verbally abusive marriage recently remarked that his divorce had finally given him his life back and now he was going to use it for God.

You may feel the same way if you have lived for years with some form of abuse. Reclaiming your life is a process. It starts when you obtain custody of yourself.

FORGET
tHE PAST.

THERE'S
NO FUTURE
iN it!

FRIENDSHIP

A friend

should bear

his friends

infirmities.

WILLIAM
SHAKESPEARE

I NEED All the FRiENds I CAN GEt!

Steve summed up most people's feelings in our workshop when he said, "I feel so ashamed that I am going through a divorce. I have let my family down, my church down, my friends down, and God down. I don't even want to be seen in public these days."

Many divorcing people want to simply sneak away to the wilderness and only reappear in public when their divorce has become ancient history. Shame, embarrassment, loss of self-esteem, and huge waves of paranoia often invade the lives of divorced men and women to the point where they want no contact with other people, except when it is mandatory to their daily survival. Although I understand these feelings, I must admit that this is not the healthiest way to survive a divorce.

One of the toughest things about a divorce is losing your support system and extended family community. Within one year of a divorce, many men and women lose up to 80 percent of the friends they had when they were married. Building a new support system in your single-again life does not happen quickly. Friendship is generally not a high priority when you

are struggling with tough divorce issues. Relationships take time and energy, both of which are hard to come by.

You need a healthy support system to provide a sense of belonging and identity for those months of transition that lie ahead. To ensure that this happens, you will have to reach out and ask for help and support. That will take a fair degree of courage on your part, but it is essential for your growth and healing.

I believe God uses new people in your life to administer healing. If you have an open and receptive spirit, God will plant people in your pathway. New friendships are often born at the place of greatest pain.

In the church where I work, I watch hurting people learn to cling to each other as they rebuild their support systems. Many tell me they have found the best friends they have ever had while their world was falling apart in a divorce.

The truth is . . . we need each other. Even Jesus recognized this when He sent His disciples out on a missionary journey. Individually they could have covered their assignment more quickly, but emotionally they needed the strength, encouragement, and support of each other to make their journey a success.

Are you living in isolation, or are you receiving strength by reaching out to people around you? Will you walk today with an open heart and open spirit to the people God will place in your pathway?

In the comic strip *Peanuts*, Good Ol' Charlie Brown expresses our deep human need when he says, "I need all the friends I can get."

I do. So do you!

WhEN You FEEl UNlovEd

The tears cascaded down her cheeks as she sobbed and gasped for air. She was the early morning recipient of the words "I don't love you anymore." Those words were followed by the inevitable: "I am in love with someone else, and I will be moving out on the weekend."

As she sat in my office, she struggled to make sense out of something that made no sense. After twenty-some years of marriage, she had grown children and financial stability, but she was about to lose it all to someone she didn't even know existed before that day. Like many others in similar aftershock, she desperately wanted to find answers to the unanswerable.

How does any human being who thought they were loved respond to the statement that they are not loved any longer? What can anyone say when they are told that the love they once felt has now been transferred to another human being?

A vast majority of the men and women going through divorce today are victims of "the affair." There may be a thousand reasons, logical or illogical, for an affair to happen, but the cruel end result is always the same. You end up rejected, feeling unloved and betrayed.

We all need acceptance, affirmation, and love. When we have it in great abundance, we thrive and grow. When it is removed, we tend to whither and die. Divorce is often said to be the death of a relationship. It can also be the death of a human spirit, and it can raise the question: "Will I ever be loved again by one special person?"

One of my favorite television programs is *Touched By An Angel*. When I watch, I wait for that magical moment on the show when the heavenly halo is ignited over the head of the angel, who then says: "God loves you. He really does."

That's the message I have for you today, my reader friend. If someone you loved has told you they do not love you anymore, you need to know that they don't speak for God. The message Jesus brought to earth and lived out was the message of love. He is your intimate friend.

Remember that verse from the Bible you learned in Sunday school? "For God so loved the world that He gave His only begotten Son, that whoever believes in Him should not perish but have everlasting life" (John 3:16). That "world" includes **you**. No matter what you think or feel today, no matter how unloved you feel . . . **You are loved by God, and you can be secure in that love.**

You are still . . . today . . . God's unique, unrepeatable miracle.

GOD LOVES DIVORCED PEOPLE!

HOW DO YOU FEEL Right Now?

She sat in the second row every week and glared back at me with a look of defiance that had the cutting ability of a blowtorch. During the third week of our divorce recovery seminar, I asked her how she was doing. She gritted out the word "fine" and stomped off to her small group. I knew she was a long way from "fine" and was doing what many other seminar participants had done over the years . . . stuffing her feelings.

Feelings surge inside of us like the tides of the ocean. We know they are there, but if we acknowledge them through verbal expression, we often fear we are admitting our weaknesses.

Psychologists tell us we have four basic feelings and a whole host of periphery feelings. The primary feelings are sad, mad, glad, and scared. (No, *exhausted* is not one of them.) At different times of the day, these basic feelings pop up with little or no warning.

In small group discussions, I often ask this question: "How do you feel about your former spouse right now?" (I usually ask this question when things are dull). It instantly evokes strong feelings and elicits a wide range of responses. The word *mad* comes up more times than *glad*.

Feelings are neither right nor wrong. They just are. We can choose to repress them or express them. God has gifted us with our feelings, and He made us with the vital need to express and share them. When we express emotions, we are free to take ownership of them. When we repress our feelings, we short-circuit our personal growth. Expressing feelings keeps us in touch with our thinking, feeling, and acting self. They allow us to respond to what is happening both inside and outside of us.

Sharing our feelings with other people is a sign of growth and strength. We usually feel better when we have shared our feelings with another person who has genuinely heard us. Even though other people cannot resolve our feelings, they have the power to receive our emotions and empathize with us. I have watched men and women share their deep feelings in our divorce support groups for over twenty-five years, and they usually tell me that they feel much better afterward.

We also need to share our feelings with God. He is able to hear our personal expressions and respond to them with His protective love. God sets you free today to share your feelings. It will cleanse your spirit and remove some of the emotional logjams in your life. Saint Paul wrote these words to the early Christians: "Where the Spirit of the Lord is, there is liberty" (2 Cor. 3:17).

Check your feelings right now. What do you need to share with a trusted friend? What do you need to share with God?

A Strategy For Survival

Divorce can bury you faster than a Minnesota blizzard in January. Hope for any relief is usually very remote. You begin to feel like you are fighting a losing battle and will soon be buried underneath a never-ending list of issues that need answers and resolutions.

Many people who are living through a divorce feel overwhelmed, overloaded, and out of control. They wonder if a day will ever arrive when they will once again feel even remotely in control of their lives and the lives of their children.

Amanda was one of those persons. She came to our divorce recovery workshop very pregnant, and her baby was due at about the time the seminar ended. She already had two young sons and was feeling the pain of desertion by her spouse. She was barely working, and her living situation with a friend was tentative and very inadequate. The problems in every area of her life were slowly beating her into submission.

Amanda began to build a friendship circle in our workshop. People began to help her in areas of urgent need. Her third son was born as her new friends rallied to support her.

Fast forward to today, four years later. Amanda is remarried to a wonderful Christian man, is expecting her fourth child, and has a successful career and a future filled with optimism and hope.

I believe that changes began to occur in her life when she realized her battle did not belong to her, but to the Lord.

The Scriptures provide a powerful example of what to do with insurmountable problems. In 2 Chronicles 20, Israel is surrounded on every side by the militant forces of a hostile nation; the people stood in fear of total annihilation. One solitary voice arose from somewhere deep in the crowd and proclaimed, "Thus says the Lord to you: 'Do not be afraid nor dismayed because of this great multitude, for the battle is not yours, but God's'" (v. 15).

A pretty simple battle plan, but it may seem highly unbelievable when we relate it to our own battles. The good news is that it worked for Israel, and it can work for you and me.

When you feel that your problems outnumber your solutions and you are caught in the crossfire, stop for a minute and realize that your battles are God's battles. He will guide you through every conflict you face. If you will just let God be God, He will walk you through life's battlefields and bring you to the side of victory.

GENUINE beginnings begin with us, EVEN WHEN they ARE brought to OUR ATTENTION by EXTERNAL opportunities.

WILLIAM BRIDGES

FRIENDSHIP
is the
iNEXPRESSible
COMFORT Of
FEELING SAFE
WITH A
PERSON,
HAVING NEITHER
TO WEIGH
THOUGHTS OR
MEASURE WORDS.

GEORGE ELLIOT

A FRIEND FOR SINGLE PARENTS

I see them every Sunday morning, wrestling their kids out of suburban utility vehicles and marching them across the church patio to Sunday school classes. Some of the children are excited to be going to class while others want to run away to the beach for the day. These families look like everyone else's, except one parent is noticeably absent. These are the numerous single parent families of our church.

Being a single parent is one of the toughest assignments any mother or father can have. With the parental workforce cut in half, there is twice as much work, and there is never enough money, time, or help. Even when divorce wars have been reduced to minor skirmishes, a parent's emotional energy never seems to recover. Most single parents work long hours for little money and pray daily for the strength to keep moving forward.

Being a single parent means facing these five personal challenges.

1. Giving your children two gifts each day: the gift of time and the gift of love.

2. Being fair with your children, even when your own situation in life is probably far from fair.

3. Being honest, even if you have been the victim of flagrant dishonesty.

4. Being strong in your role as a parent, despite the temptation to throw up your hands in frustration and despair and run away from home.

5. Giving your children the freedom to be children in the midst of some very adult problems and situations.

I have personally watched many single mothers and fathers become wonderful parents. They are confident that their children can fulfill their dreams in spite of the trauma and chaos caused by divorce.

If you have children and find yourself in the role of a single parent today, rest assured that God's arms are long enough to wrap around your entire family. He can keep them secure, protected, and well loved.

SINGLE PARENT'S PRAYER

Lord, grant me the time enough to do all the chores, join in all the games, help with the lessons, say the night prayers, and still have a few moments left for myself.

Lord, grant me energy enough to be bread baker and breadwinner, knee patcher and peacemaker, ballplayer and bill juggler.

Lord, grant me hands enough to wipe away tears, to reach out when I'm needed, to hug and to hold, to tickle and to touch.

Lord, grant me heart enough to share and to care, to listen and to do, to understand and to make a loving home for my family.

Amen.

ANONYMOUS SINGLE PARENT

GROWING STRONG AT BROKEN PLACES

She had all of the qualifications necessary to join the band of the walking wounded. Her husband's affair had ended a forty-year marriage. During those forty years she had attained public recognition and numerous accolades for her work with children in the religious community. Now she was alone and very distraught, and her much-loved home was on the real estate market. Many of her life-long friends had turned their backs on her, proclaiming she was the cause of the problem because she wasn't spiritual enough.

When I met her, she said she could not go on. Most of her days were tear-filled and empty. For months we encouraged her to attend our divorce recovery workshop, but she continually refused, saying it would do no good.

She finally gave in and came to the workshop armed with a box of tissue and sat in a seat in the very back row. Week after week, she cried her way through the teaching times and small group experiences while loudly proclaiming there was no hope for her.

Then a miracle happened!

The tears began to dry up, a small smile appeared, and with the help of her support group, she began to believe that there was a life for her after divorce. Today, she has a wonderful job and a huge new circle of friends, and she is consistently one of the happiest people in our church family.

I believe she has learned to live out the principle statements of two people. The first is Ernest Hemingway, who said, "Life breaks us all sometimes, but some grow strong at the broken places." Even more significant are the words of Saint Paul, who wrote, "When I am weak, then I am strong" (2 Cor. 12:10).

When a marriage is broken by divorce, the pain can sear your very soul and push you to the brink as you surrender all hope for your future. Turning your brokenness into strength is a choice. With God's help, you can give Him your weakness and then receive the strength He offers you.

Divorce can break you, but you are never beyond repair with God!

I Just Want to Belong Somewhere

*B*ill felt so unwanted after a long and bitter divorce that he went to a video dating service. After some very forgettable dates and a fair expenditure of money, he moved along to computer dating. Cyberspace connections ended up as disappointing as the video variety. He spent a few months in computer chat rooms until he ran out of mundane conversations. By the time he got into my office, he was relationally exhausted and firmly convinced he would never belong to and be a special part of someone else's life again. He loudly proclaimed, "I just don't belong anywhere."

Does that sound familiar?

It is extremely difficult to leave the security of belonging to another person in marriage and then begin to mix with all the other human traffic on the single-again freeway. Self-doubts can become overpowering obstacles in the search for belonging.

For years, I have observed first-time visitors to our singles groups. The look on their face says they do not want to be in the room with other people who probably don't want to be in the same room with them either. They are tentative and hesitant, and they want to make sure they know where all the exits are. When they walk in, they don't feel like they belong, no matter how warm and caring the people inside are.

I remember one lady telling me that she knew she belonged when she found out where the restrooms were, could find the coffee table, and had a correctly spelled nametag. I wish belonging were that easy for everyone.

Remember your first day of school as a child? Everything was scary and threatening. You wanted to run home to the things you knew and trusted. After a few weeks, your uncertainty was replaced by a sense of belonging and school roared along. When that new kid moved to town in the middle of the year and entered your classroom, you were the pro because you were there first and you really belonged.

It's tough to be the new kid when you are thirty-five, forty-five, or fifty-five. It takes time and some serious adjustments to belong to any new group of people. But it sure beats feeling like you don't belong.

Starting over means looking for a place to belong. If you are willing to make the attempt, it will be worth the pain of trying. Everyone needs to know that they belong somewhere. Where do you feel you belong today? Who do you feel you belong with? Are you willing to start reaching out to others?

Tough Questions... Tougher Answers

The phone call was like many I receive. The feelings and questions tumbled over each other at machine gun speed. They came from a voice filled with fear and panic as an about-to-be single mother struggled with her immediate future.

I brought her monologue to a brief halt and asked her to make an appointment with me so we could talk at length in my office.

When she appeared a few days later, we were able to condense her questions down to four basic ones. They are the four questions we all ask when faced with a crisis of any proportion.

1. How will I survive and make it through this situation?
2. Where can I get help if I need it?
3. How will this affect the rest of my life?
4. Where is God in all this?

These may be your questions today, and you may be frantically searching everywhere for the answers. You may have already answered them by simply saying, "I don't know." But that answer isn't giving you peace and comfort.

There are two kinds of answers to these questions. One is practical, and the other is spiritual. Though there really aren't any universal answers to fit everyone's situation, people who have walked in similar shoes on a very similar pathway can share why and how they have learned to navigate the rapids of Divorce Country.

The spiritual answer begins when you entrust your questions to God, knowing that He will care for you.

One of my favorite Bible verses is found in Jeremiah 29:11: "For I know the thoughts that I think toward you, says the Lord, thoughts of peace and not of evil, to give you a future and a hope." It translates to four things God will do for you: Prosper you, protect you, provide for you, and prepare for your future. As you struggle with those four questions, consider these four promises from God.

It is important that you know that God will guide you through the scary places. His promise is that you will never be alone in those places. You will form some scar tissue on your soul and spirit that will always remind you of what you have come through, but you can wear those scars as symbols of your trust in God and His faithfulness to you.

Pray this simple prayer today: "God, stay close to me when I have to walk in hard places. May any scars I acquire from this journey only make me stronger."

The Questions of Growth and Change

1. Who Am I? This question is both simple and complex. It has to do with your identity, not someone else's. During and after a divorce, many men and women begin to question who they are. They sometimes realize that their former spouse either erased or stole their identity.

2. Where Am I Going? This question involves taking a long look at your future, setting some goals, and deciding who will walk that journey with you.

3. How Will I Get There? You will need to decide if your vehicle of change will be vocational, educational, or geographical.

4. Who Will Help Me? What kind of people do you need around you as you move in new directions? Do you need to replace some unsupportive people with some healthy and nourishing ones?

5. Am I Willing to Take the Risk? To risk is to sometimes fail and at other times succeed. There are no guarantees when you take risks.

When God
shuts a door,
He opens
a window.

John Ruskin

REGAINING TRUST

We were talking about trust in a seminar. Afterwards, a woman came up to me and said, "One of the good things about my post-divorce life is that the pain of my marriage break-up is gone. I don't hurt as much as I once did, and I am learning to trust people again." She probably expressed the feelings that many in the workshop were experiencing. It is not easy to regain trust when someone you loved broke that trust.

The pain from broken trust can be carried for years after a divorce if the healing process is denied. Broken trust makes a person bitter, angry, and vengeful. Even if only one person broke your trust, every other person on the planet of the same sex is then looked upon as untrustworthy.

Healing a broken trust starts by realizing that everyone else is not your former spouse. Hurt is often person-centered. When that person becomes more distant in your life and is no longer a primary focus, the seeds of healing can begin to grow.

Renewing your trust begins by reaching out to other people and taking a risk. All relationships are a risk, and they hold no guarantees. Can you be hurt again? Yes! Will you be hurt again? Probably! Remember that Jesus was hurt by those closest to Him. Simon Peter led the parade, but Jesus did not close the door because He understood that people are human and that they sometimes make bad decisions.

Broken relationships and broken trust can hang like a heavy weight around your neck. You can probably identify with the Psalmist when he says, "My soul melts from heaviness; strengthen me according to Your word" (Ps. 119:28).

Renewing trust is a process. It happens ever so slowly, but it does happen.

Without forgiveness, life is governed by an endless cycle of resentment and retaliation.

ROBERT ASSAGLIOLI

God tempers
the wind
to the
shorn lamb.

LAURENCE STERNE

SMALL TALK WITH A BIG GOD

*I*t was a gift at the end of the seminar I conducted in a distant city. The lady giving it to me said, "Read this on your way home. It will make you laugh a lot." I opened her gift book on the airplane and was captured by the title, *Lord, I Said*. Each page contained a cartoon of a stick figure talking to a cloud that represented God. The one that really stopped me cold showed the little stick figure looking at the cloud and saying, "'Lord,' I said, 'why didn't I leave things in your hands?' The answer came back, 'You keep forgetting,' He said, 'which one of us is God.'"

Have you forgotten that lately? It is pretty easy to take things into our own hands when we should be leaving them in God's hands. Most of us try to do everything ourselves and only give God the 17 percent we can't figure out. Then when our 83 percent gets really messed up, we wonder where God is.

It is hard to trust God with the little things. It is even harder to trust Him with the big things. Somehow we feel that the creator of the universe is just not up to our challenges, or

we are fearful that God will bring some kind of perverse misery on us if we really put Him in charge of our struggles.

One of the biggest struggles in Divorce Country is to believe that ANYONE cares at all about what you are going through. Families can desert you. Friends can avoid you when they see you coming. Your children can tell you that everything that happened is your fault. Well-meaning spiritual friends can quote all the Scriptures on divorce to you. And you wonder if anyone really cares about YOU.

When no one seems to care, remember God cares. Remember there is a great promise in 1 Peter 5:7: "Casting all your care upon Him for He cares for you." Whatever your cares and concerns are, you can be assured that when you give them to God, He will take care of you.

I will not FEAR, FOR you ARE EVER with me, AND you will NEVER leave me to FACE my perils alone.

THOMAS MERTON

SEARCHING FOR THE WORDS

ears filled his eyes, and he looked like he was on the edge of a total meltdown. He had wandered into our church in hopes of finding some way to make an impending divorce disappear.

As I listened to his long and sad tale of a thirty-year marriage about to dissolve, I found myself searching for the words that would make the tears cease and a smile surface.

I counsel, I write books, I conduct seminars. I know how to use words to ease pain and instill a glimmer of hope in people's lives. As the minutes ticked by and our church auditorium was left with only the cleaning crew moving around, I found myself totally empty of any words that could edge him from despair into optimism.

I ended up resorting to the two things that I know I can always do. Pray and then schedule an appointment with him during the coming week.

I felt sad as I watched him walk away across our church patio, with sagging shoulders, a sagging heart, and a sagging spirit. I desperately wanted to shout words of hope into his life and tell him that thousands of others just like him had survived bitter divorces and found new life on the other side of Divorce Country.

I knew he would have to walk through the valley of pain to reach the mountaintop of recovery. You may have to do the same thing on your journey.

No one, no matter how deeply they care about you, can reverse your life processes and send you in a new direction. The best we can do for those who are in deep pain is grab their hand, hold on tightly, walk with them, and pray for them.

Words usually fail to stop the flood of thoughts, emotions, and feelings. Knowing that you are not alone in what you face, that someone stands with you, can bring the dawn of hope back into your life.

Sometimes the people God brings to us when we feel overwhelmed by hurt and pain are true miracle workers. They come to us through strange circumstances when we least expect them. God somehow seems to always know what we need — He knows we need people more than words.

Do you need someone to stand with you today as you try to navigate your way through the rapids of divorce? Are you willing to ask God to send that person to you?

The Bible tells us that whenever God wanted to get something done, He called a special person to do it. I believe that God can bring His special person into your life to walk with you today.

Your prayer can be simple: "Lord, send someone to help me through this!"

Then, keep your eyes open for that person.

BRING YOUR OWN CHEERLEADERS

Have you ever watched cheerleaders at a high school football game? It doesn't matter if their team is winning or losing, they still keep cheering until the final gun sounds. Even if their team has lost ten games in a row and is in last place in the standings, they still cheer.

It is a lot easier to cheer for a winning team than a losing team. Losers don't generate a lot of enthusiasm, and they don't bring trophies back to campus at the end of the season. Maybe only winning teams should have cheerleaders. Do you even need cheerleaders when you are winning?

I believe everyone needs a few cheerleaders in life. You, me, and the guy next door. Divorced people and married people, single people and unsingle people. Little kids and big kids, company presidents and janitors. We all need someone, somewhere cheering for us because we don't always win.

Who cheers for you while you pick your way through the minefields of Divorce Country? Your mom and dad and your kids? Your office friends and bowling team? Your minister and ushers at church? No one? Divorced people often find that those who once cheered for them now have joined the "boo birds" on the sidelines.

God has a unique way of giving you a new cheerleading squad when the old ones have disappeared. Some of your new cheerleaders will be other people who have gone through a divorce and understand your struggles. Don't be afraid to go looking for them.

You may find a few of them around your church, your neighborhood, at work, at the supermarket, at your hair stylist, or at your favorite coffeehouse. They usually don't advertise their presence. They tend to just appear at your side when you least expect them. They may be young, or they may be older than you. They may dress fashionably or weirdly.

Before you know it, you will have assembled your own cheerleading squad. Everybody needs one, so keep your megaphone and pompom handy!

I Am Loved

I had just finished a seminar in a distant city and was anxious to get to the airport and fly home. A lady stopped me as I was leaving the seminar and asked me if she could pin something on my blazer. I said yes, and she pinned it to me as I hurried to my transportation.

Waiting in the airport, I glanced down to read the pin. A bright red circle with white lettering said, "I AM LOVED." My inner response was, I *know that*. My wife loves me, my children love me, God loves me, and a scattered assortment of friends love me. I was surrounded by people who loved me, and that feeling made me secure.

Then I thought about other people who might have trouble wearing that pin. Many people feel unloved and might want to wear a pin that says, "I AM NOT LOVED." It would certainly attract a lot of attention but very little love.

The words I *love you* have a way of leading two people to the altar of marriage. The words I *don't love you anymore* can land someone in the middle of Divorce Country. It is amazing how one's life can change when love dies. Loss of self-esteem and self-love are usually close behind.

Years ago, I encouraged men and women in our workshops to stand at the end and say out loud, "God loves me. I am His unique, unrepeatable miracle!" Very few said it above a whisper because they personally doubted that they could be loved when the one they loved rejected them.

To be healthy and whole, we need to know we are loved by those around us. When human love is scarce, we have to take the promise of Scripture and let it warm our heart. Take a moment right now and say out loud, "God loves me! He really loves me!" Forget those who do not love you and focus on those who do!

RELYING ON GOD HAS TO BEGIN ALL OVER AGAIN EVERY DAY AS IF NOTHING HAD YET BEEN DONE.

C. S. LEWIS

LEARNING TO EMBRACE COMMITMENTS

"'ll never marry again!" she said. "A marriage ceremony is where promises are made, married life is where they are lived out, and a divorce is where they are broken." After uttering those words, she closed the door and disappeared down my hallway. I wondered how many times I had heard similar comments from a bruised and broken man or woman.

Many look back on an unhappy marriage where commitments were not kept and decide that they will never make any commitments again. They become "commitment shy" in many areas of their lives because they have been hurt.

It is easy to build a shrine around your hurt and spend the rest of your life worshipping it. Broken commitments in your past must not keep you from making new commitments in your future. If we learn from the past, then past failures will not lead to future failures.

The fear of failure keeps many men and women from new commitments in the areas of job changes, career goals, geographical relocation, daily responsibilities, and new friendships. The bottom line is simple: They don't want to be hurt again, and they don't want to fail. The reality of living on this planet is that we will be hurt at times, and we will fail at times. This is the only way we can grow because we learn from our experiences.

Making any new commitment is not easy. It becomes a decision of the mind, will, and emotions. It can only be lived out by the person making it. Being a responsive and responsible adult means owning and living up to your commitments.

As you take new, tiny steps in commitment today, know that God is with you and His promise from the Psalms is for you: "I will instruct you and teach you in the way you should go; I will guide you with My eye" (32:8). You always have to wait for the instructions before you start a journey — ask for God's guidance.

HAPPY ARE
those who
dREAM dREAMs
ANd ARE REAdy
to pAy the
pRicE to
mAKE thEm
COmE tRUE.

L. J. CARDINAL
SUENENS

NOW, ABOUT THE REST OF YOUR LIFE

I would like to think that I have woven some thread of hope and renewal for you throughout this short book. But none of the words of encouragement and growth will mean much to you unless you make them a part of your daily journey through Divorce Country. Thousands, yes millions, have walked that pathway before you. Sadly, many will come after you, and they too will wonder if they can survive and rebuild a life with meaning and purpose in it.

A wise person once said that there are three things that give meaning and purpose to our lives: **(1) Something to do! (2) Someone to love! (3) Something to look forward to!** Divorce has a way of either attempting to permanently destroy those things or put them on hold indefinitely.

I believe you need to work on them every day of your life — starting now. Find meaningful things to do that give something back to you. Find people in your life that you can love. Make plans for your future. Remember, you have to live your life and what you do today will influence how you choose to live tomorrow.

You may think that this is fairy dust, and that it doesn't apply to your life today.

I have worked in the divorce recovery field for over twenty-five years, and I have watched firsthand as hurting people slowly puttheir lives back together. I have watched miracles great and small take place as many men and women regained balance, meaning, and purpose. So it's not fairy dust!

As I have said to thousands of people over the years, you always have a choice. You can go through it, or you can **grow through it**.

My prayer for you today is that you will choose to GROW and that your life will forever be changed by that growth.

In the present, every day is a miracle.

JAMES GOULD
COZZENS

HOW TO SURVIVE A DIVORCE

TEN things to do when you FEEl A divorce is iNEvitAble:

1. When the reality of a divorce hits you, stop long enough to commit your entire situation to God through prayer, and ask Him to provide help, guidance, and emotional support.

2. Call your best friends and ask them for their prayers and emotional support.

3. Stay in touch with your feelings and share them with people you can trust.

4. Don't blame God for your divorce or criticize Him for His seeming inability to prevent it.

5. Don't panic. Remember, no matter what happens, God is still in charge.

6. Contact an attorney to find out about your legal grounds.

7. Make a list of all your fears. Then make a list of all your resources.

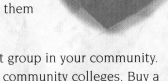

8. Gather as many members of your family around you as you can. Ask them for their love and support.

9. Seek out a divorce support group in your community. These often meet in churches and community colleges. Buy a copy of *Growing Through Divorce* and read it many times.

10. Remember that healing takes time. There is no quick fix for a divorce.